RIVERS AND STREAMS

A Buddy Book
by
Fran Howard

ABDO
Publishing Company

VISIT US AT

www.abdopublishing.com

Published by ABDO Publishing Company, 4940 Viking Drive, Edina, Minnesota 55435.

Copyright © 2007 by Abdo Consulting Group, Inc. International copyrights reserved in all countries. No part of this book may be reproduced in any form without written permission from the publisher. Buddy Books™ is a trademark and logo of ABDO Publishing Company.

Printed in the United States.

Edited by: Sarah Tieck
Contributing Editor: Michael P. Goecke
Graphic Design: Brady Wise
Image Research: Deb Coldiron, Maria Hosley, Heather Sagisser, Brady Wise
Photographs: Corbis, Flat Earth, Minden Pictures, Photodisc, photos.com

Library of Congress Cataloging-in-Publication Data

Howard, Fran, 1953-
    Rivers and streams / Fran Howard.
        p. cm. — (Habitats)
    Includes bibliographical references and index.
    ISBN 1-59679-782-7 (10 digit ISBN)
    ISBN 978-1-59679-782-6 (13 digit ISBN)
        1. Rivers—Juvenile literature. I. Title. II. Series: Habitats (Edina, Minn.)

QH97.H69 2006
577.6'4—dc22

                                                                    2005031602

TABLE OF CONTENTS

What Are Rivers and Streams?

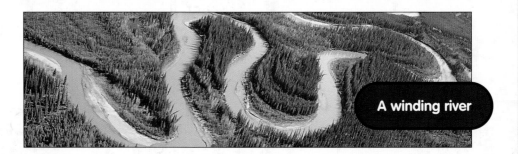

A winding river

Rivers and streams are flowing bodies of **freshwater**. The water in rivers and streams comes from rain, snow, and other sources. Streams are smaller than rivers.

Some streams begin high in the mountains. Streams join rivers. Rivers flow into the oceans.

Rivers and streams are types of habitats. Habitats are the places where plants and animals find food, water, and places to live.

Different plants and animals live in different habitats. There are a lot of plants and animals that live in or by rivers and streams.

The gray wolf is one animal that lives by rivers.

WHERE ARE RIVERS AND STREAMS FOUND?

This river is in a forest.

Rivers and streams are found all over the world. They flow through forests, mountains, and even deserts.

A moving stream

Moving rivers and streams can be found on most **continents**. Only Antarctica does not have moving rivers and streams. This is because Antarctica is very cold. Antarctica's rivers and streams are frozen.

The Nile River in Africa is the world's longest river. It is 4,160 miles (6,695 km) long. The second-longest river in the world is the Amazon River in South America.

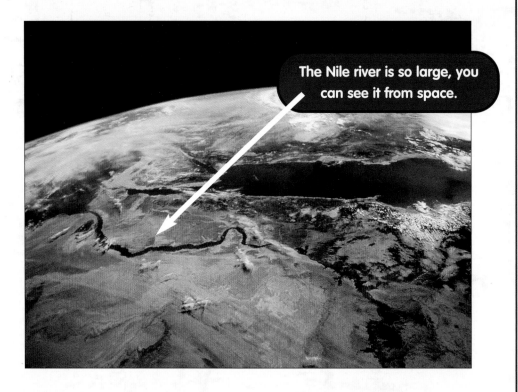

The Nile river is so large, you can see it from space.

PLANTS OF
RIVERS AND STREAMS

Trees and plants grow by rivers.

Plants live in and by rivers and streams. Some plants grow in the water. Trees grow on the banks of rivers and streams. Other plants grow on the muddy riverbanks, too.

Giant water lily pads

The giant water lily is a plant that grows in the Amazon River. This water lily's pad can grow to be more than two feet (one m) wide.

Lily pads grow in the water.

WATER ANIMALS OF
RIVERS AND STREAMS

Many kinds of animals live in and by rivers and streams. Some of these are fish, snakes, and shrimps.

Bullheads are a type of fish that live in rivers and streams. Bullheads have flat heads. This allows them to push under rocks. Bullheads eat from the bottom of rivers and streams.

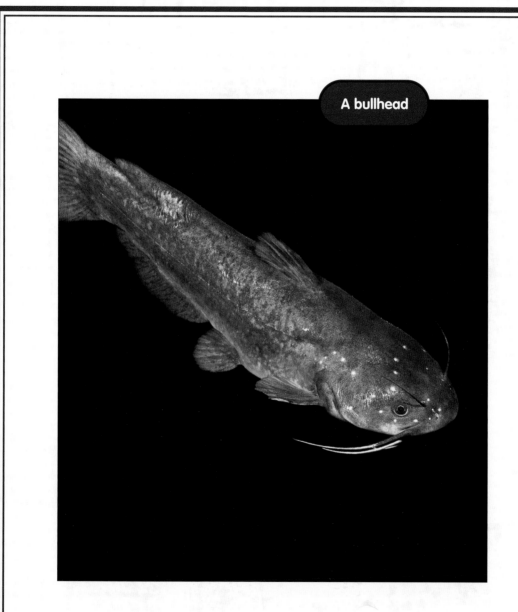

A bullhead

Some animals use rivers and streams as travel routes. Salmon are fish that travel in rivers and streams.

These salmon are swimming up the river. They often swim against the current.

Young salmon live in the river for two or three years. Then, they swim to the ocean.

Years later, the salmon return to the rivers where they were born. Some salmon swim many miles in a day.

At the end of the long trip, they lay their eggs. Young salmon **hatch** from the eggs. And the **cycle** starts all over again.

LAND ANIMALS OF
RIVERS AND STREAMS

Some animals live both on the land and in the water.

Beavers are both land and water animals. They create dams in rivers and streams using logs, mud, and plants. These dams provide shelter for beavers.

A beaver

River otters also live both on land and in water. They like to play. They use the riverbank as a slide. But, river otters are good divers and skilled hunters, too. They hunt for small animals on land. They hunt for fish in the water.

A river otter

The platypus lives in rivers and streams in Australia. It has webbed feet and a bill like a duck. The platypus lives on land and hunts underwater. It hunts with its eyes and ears closed. This stops water from getting in. The platypus uses its bill to find food.

An Australian platypus

One bird that lives by rivers and streams is the dipper. Dippers eat water bugs, tiny fish, and fish eggs. They stand in water to hunt. Dippers sometimes dive to the bottom of the river to find food, too.

An American dipper

A white-throated dipper

Snakes also live near the river waters. The biggest river snake is the anaconda. It can grow to be 30 feet (nine m) long. That is taller than some houses!

An anaconda snake

WHY ARE RIVER AND STREAM HABITATS IMPORTANT?

People and animals need rivers and streams. Rivers and streams carry water to the ocean.

People eat fish from rivers and streams. Rivers also supply people with water.

Rivers are waterways for boats. Boats carry goods and people from place to place.

Some people ride in small boats on rivers.

Barges are large boats that carry goods on rivers.

Rivers also give people **power**. And, farmers use rivers and streams to water their crops.

Animals and plants of rivers and streams need each other. Together they form a **food chain**. Even the smallest plants and animals are part of the food chain.

Plants and animals of rivers and streams cannot live without their habitat.

River Otter   Bullhead   Shrimp

RIVERS AND STREAMS

- The Okavango River in Africa does not flow to the sea. It empties into a swamp in the Kalahari Desert.

- The Mississippi River is the longest river in the United States. It is also one of the longest rivers in the world.

- Tigers swim in the Ganges River.

- Giant river snakes called anacondas can swallow animals as big as a pig.

- Crocodiles live in the Nile River. They sometimes store food under rocks to eat later.

IMPORTANT WORDS

continent one of seven large landmasses on earth.

cycle a complete set of events that keep happening in the same order.

food chain the order in which plants and animals feed on each other.

freshwater water that does not contain salt.

hatch to be born from an egg.

power a form of energy. Electricity.

WEB SITES

Would you like to learn more about **rivers and streams**? Please visit ABDO Publishing Company on the World Wide Web to find Web site links about **rivers and streams**. These links are routinely monitored and updated to provide the most current information available.

www.abdopublishing.com

INDEX